W9-BZG-533

FRANKLIN DELANO
ROOSEVELT

THE NEW DEAL PRESIDENT

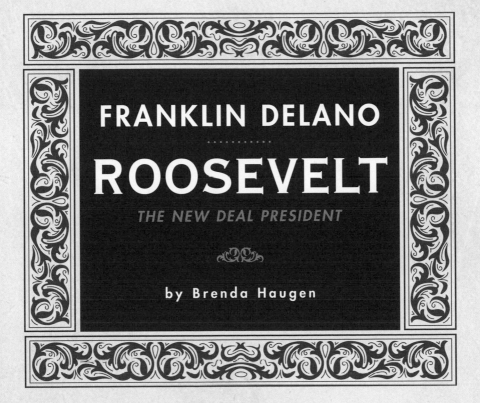

FRANKLIN DELANO
ROOSEVELT

THE NEW DEAL PRESIDENT

by Brenda Haugen

Content Adviser: James Wolfinger, Ph.D,
Assistant Professor, Department of History,
DePaul University

Reading Adviser: Rosemary G. Palmer, Ph.D.,
Department of Literacy, College of Education,
Boise State University

COMPASS POINT BOOKS ✶ MINNEAPOLIS, MINNESOTA

Compass Point Books
3109 West 50th Street, #115
Minneapolis, MN 55410

Visit Compass Point Books on the Internet at *www.compasspointbooks.com*
or e-mail your request to *custserv@compasspointbooks.com*

Editor: Shelly Lyons
Page Production: Heather Griffin
Photo Researcher: Marcie C. Spence
Cartographer: XNR Productions
Library Consultant: Kathleen Baxter

Art Director: Jaime Martens
Creative Director: Keith Griffin
Editorial Director: Carol Jones
Managing Editor: Catherine Neitge

*I dedicate this book to the memory of my grandmother, Bernadine
Kingston. If I can be even half the person she was, I will consider my life a
great success. BLH*

Library of Congress Cataloging-in-Publication Data
Haugen, Brenda.
 Franklin Delano Roosevelt : the New Deal president / by Brenda Haugen.
   p. cm. — (Signature lives)
 Includes bibliographical references and index.
 ISBN 0-7565-1586-6 (hard cover)
 1. Roosevelt, Franklin D. (Franklin Delano), 1882-1945—Juvenile litera-
ture. 2. Presidents—United States—Biography—Juvenile literature. I. Title.
II. Series.
 E807.H365 2006
 973.917092—dc22   2005027142

MODERN AMERICA

Starting in the late 19th century, advancements in all areas of human activity transformed an old world into a new and modern place. Inventions prompted rapid shifts in lifestyle, and scientific discoveries began to alter the way humanity viewed itself. Beginning with World War I, warfare took place on a global scale, and ideas such as nationalism and communism showed that countries were taking a larger view of their place in the world. The combination of all these changes continues to produce what we know as the modern world.

Table of Contents

1 A Big Bump in the Road

❧❦❧

Franklin D. Roosevelt feared fire his whole life, but he also loved the outdoors, especially around his vacation home on Campobello Island, Canada. On August 10, 1921, Roosevelt left the family cabin on Campobello Island, to go sailing on the boat *Vireo* with his children. He had been tired even before arriving on his vacation, and his journey to the island had proved difficult. However, sailing ranked as one of his favorite pastimes, and he wouldn't let fatigue stand in the way of having fun with his children.

Suddenly, they noticed plumes of smoke rising in the distance. A forest fire blazed on a small island near them. Even though he feared fire, he didn't hesitate to help fight it. Roosevelt and his children sailed across the water and fought the blaze by pounding the flames

Franklin Delano Roosevelt loved to sail, especially in the water surrounding Campobello Island, Canada.

Canada is one of the largest countries in the world, second only to Russia in land mass. Much of the country is sparsely populated, however, because of its rugged terrain and cold temperatures. Nearly three out of four Canadians live within 100 miles (160 kilometers) of the country's southern border.

with evergreen branches they'd cut themselves.

"It was a terrifying sight," Roosevelt's daughter, Anna, remembered. "And it was a terrifying feeling to be standing next to a fir tree, suddenly have it catch fire, and hear the awful roar of the flames as they enveloped the whole tree."

Once the fire was out, the Roosevelts, exhausted and dirty, sailed back to Campobello Island. Roosevelt suggested they all go for a swim to clean off the grime, and he led a 2-mile (3-kilometer) jog across the island to a freshwater pond. There they romped around in the cold water.

Clean but tired, Roosevelt and the children returned to their cabin. The children went to put on dry clothes, but Roosevelt decided to read the newspaper before changing out of his wet swimsuit. By the time he finished his reading, he felt chilled and tired, so he chose to go to bed early instead of dining with the family.

During the night, Roosevelt rose to use the bathroom, but his legs didn't seem to work. His wife, Eleanor, found him crawling on his hands and knees.

The next morning, he appeared to be his normal, cheerful self. He even cracked jokes with Anna. However, he ate breakfast in bed. His left leg didn't want to support him when he tried to get up. "I tried to persuade myself that this trouble with my leg was muscular, that it would disappear as I used it," Roosevelt recalled. "But presently, it refused to work, and then the other."

In 1918, Franklin D. Roosevelt was a healthy husband and father, but just three years later, polio struck his body and left its mark.

Eleanor contacted a country doctor to examine her husband. Dr. E.H. Bennett thought Roosevelt was just suffering from a bad cold. But when Roosevelt's health grew worse, Bennett was stumped. He couldn't explain Roosevelt's severe leg and back pain. In a couple of weeks, his suffering intensified. He couldn't move any of the muscles below his chest, though the pain there persisted. His temperature shot up to 102 degrees Fahrenheit (39 degrees Celsius). Even the weight of the bedsheets caused him terrible anguish.

A combination of pain and numbness spread throughout Roosevelt's shoulders, arms, and fingers.

Normal human body temperature is around 98.6 degrees Fahrenheit (37 degrees Celsius). When a person has a fever, it can be a signal of disease. The brain raises the body's temperature to help fight viruses and bacteria. The higher temperature makes the body a less comfortable place for the viruses to be. However, a fever higher than 103 ℉ (39.4 C) can cause harm to a person's brain.

His friend and political adviser, Louis Howe, worked with Bennett to find a specialist who might be able to help. They found a Philadelphia doctor, William Keen, who was vacationing at a resort in nearby Maine. Keen agreed to examine Roosevelt, but he couldn't diagnose the problem either. He thought there might be a blood clot in Roosevelt's spine, so he prescribed massage, an order Eleanor followed faithfully.

When Roosevelt's suffering continued, another specialist, Dr. Robert Lovett, was called. After examining Roosevelt, Lovett gave a diagnosis that shocked everyone—infantile paralysis, also known as polio. Until Lovett arrived, no one really even thought of polio because it was considered a disease that only struck children. Roosevelt's son James remembered:

We all were shocked. Mother's first reaction was panic. She wondered what would happen to them and their lives. Then she feared for the health of her children. However, Dr. Lovett decided that if we had not already shown symptoms of the disease and were kept in quarantine away from father, we probably would be all right.

Apparently Roosevelt had come in contact with the polio virus and, because of his recent strenuous activities, was unable to fight it off. However, Lovett believed Roosevelt would get better, though it might take months.

Roosevelt kept up hope for at least a partial recovery, but it didn't happen. He would never walk again without leg braces and support. Eventually, he would be confined to a wheelchair.

Virtually overnight, 39-year-old Roosevelt went from being strong and athletic to paralyzed and bedridden. He could have let his disability get the better of him. He could have followed the path his mother, Sara, wanted for him. She urged him to lead a life of leisure on the family's estate in New York. Instead, Roosevelt chose to continue living a life of public service. He would serve as governor of New York and later be elected president of the United States during one of the most turbulent times in the nation's history. His determination to overcome his physical disabilities would later be reflected in his determination to overcome some of the nation's most difficult times.

Roosevelt was elected president four times and served longer than any other in history. When he first took office, the country stood in the midst of the Great Depression, the greatest economic crisis the United States had ever faced. Millions of people were unemployed. Many were homeless and starving. The situation grew worse when dust storms and drought struck the country's heartland and food supply, causing the Dust Bowl.

With his New Deal programs, Roosevelt made sweeping changes to bring immediate aid to those

The Dust Bowl was created by a series of destructive dust storms that tore through the Great Plains and Southwest states from 1935 to 1938. The storms destroyed more than 50 million acres (20 million hectares) of land and would often reduce visibility to less than a mile. These storms were some of the worst natural disasters in U.S. history.

Roosevelt as governor of New York in 1930

who were suffering. The work Roosevelt did during the Great Depression saved a desperate nation. Yet it wouldn't be the only challenge he would face. Around the same time Roosevelt was first elected president, a man named Adolf Hitler came to power in Germany. The world watched as Hitler conquered numerous countries in a quest to create a German empire across much of Europe. The September 1939 invasion of Poland marked the beginning of World War II. Though most Americans wanted to stay out of the war, Roosevelt knew it would only be a matter of time before the United States would become part of it. ℘

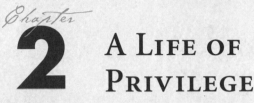

2 A LIFE OF PRIVILEGE

❦

James Roosevelt's wife, Sara, had gone into labor on January 29, 1882. After a day of enduring horrible pain, she still hadn't given birth, and James begged the doctor to do something. Seeing their distress, the doctor gave Sara a dose of chloroform in a cone placed over her face. When the first dose didn't help, the doctor gave Sara more, but it proved to be too much. Suddenly, her lips turned blue. She lost consciousness and slipped into a coma.

Terror tugged at James' heart. He feared he would lose both Sara and his unborn baby. He already had lost one wife, Rebecca Howland Roosevelt, in 1876. They had a son, also named James, who now was in his 20s and had a family of his own. About four years after Rebecca's death, the elder James married

As a young boy, Franklin Delano Roosevelt was taught to enjoy nature and animals. His father taught him to ride horses, and his grandfather taught him to sail.

Sara Delano, who, at 26, was half her husband's age. Because of James' age, the couple had decided they would only have one child together. Now it looked as if both Sara and the child would die.

But Sara emerged from the coma and gave birth to Franklin on January 30 at Springwood, the Roosevelt family estate near Hyde Park, New York. Franklin, however, looked sickly from the effects of the chloroform. His skin was blue, and he appeared groggy. "The nurse said she never expected the baby to be alive and was surprised to find that he was," Sara said.

Franklin proved to be strong, and he eventually got better. However, coming up with a name for the baby posed the next challenge. James wanted to call him Isaac, after his father. However, Sara hated that name and wanted to call him Warren Delano, after her own father. Sara's brother Warren Delano Jr. didn't side with his sister. His son, also named Warren Delano, had recently died. Warren told his sister it would cause him great pain to hear another youngster called by the same name. Sara respected that, but she wouldn't agree to Isaac. For two months, the child

Sara Delano married James Roosevelt on October 7, 1880. She had grown up in a wealthy family and with her marriage, entered another. After the birth of her son, Sara wanted to take on all the responsibilities of a mother, but many wealthy families relied heavily on nannies.

Franklin and his mother, Sara, were always close. Even after Franklin married and had children, Sara continued to be very involved in his life.

was simply called Baby. Finally, on March 20, the baby was christened Franklin Delano Roosevelt, after Sara's favorite uncle.

Franklin grew up in a wealthy family and never

wanted for anything. Sara had always lived a life of
luxury and inherited more than $1 million when her
father died. She spoiled her son by showering him
with attention and gifts. She also loved to travel with
him. By the time Franklin turned 15, he'd already
visited Europe eight times.

James Roosevelt had graduated from Harvard

*James and
Sara Roosevelt
and their son,
Franklin*

Law School, though he worked as a businessman rather than as a lawyer. Springwood kept him busy. It included 1,300 acres (520 hectares) of crops and land for cattle and horses. In his free time, James taught Franklin to swim, fish, and sail.

Franklin also owned his own horse and became a good rider. As soon as he grew old enough, he joined his father on daily rounds of the farm. Franklin's father taught him to love the land and wild animals. From his Grandpa Delano, Franklin developed a love for boats and the sea. After he turned 16, Franklin got his own boat, the *New Moon.* He enjoyed exploring the shoreline of the Bay of Fundy near Campobello Island, Canada, where his family owned a summer home.

James counted many important people among his friends. One of them was President Grover Cleveland, whom young Franklin visited with his father at the White House.

Though his parents loved him and showered him with affection, Franklin grew up in the care of governesses, as was expected of children in wealthy families. The only thing missing was contact with other youngsters. Few children his age lived or spent time

Located off the east coast of Canada, the Bay of Fundy remains a vacation attraction today. Popular for its beautiful beaches and dramatic cliffs, the bay is home to a variety of wildlife, including the endangered Northern Atlantic right whale.

near Springwood. Because his half-brother, James, was more than 20 years older than he, Franklin was never close to him. However, sometimes Franklin played with James' children when they came to visit.

Franklin spent his free time reading. The Roosevelts had a beautiful library in their home. Books about the sea and the Navy ranked among young Franklin's favorites and remained so the rest of his life.

After Franklin turned 6, he started his formal education. A governess taught him how to speak and write German. When Franklin turned 14, James convinced Sara that Franklin should leave home to attend school. Though James was sad to see him leave, he felt it was best for his son. In 1896, Franklin headed to Groton, Massachusetts, about 35 miles (56 km) north of Boston.

Boarding school proved to be a new experience for Franklin. He went from being the center of his parents' attention to being just one of the boys. Located on a grassy plateau above the Nashua River, the secluded Groton included a schoolhouse, dorm, gym, chapel, and a few other buildings. A small room with a curtain for a door served as Franklin's home at Groton. Students followed a strict schedule of classes and worship. They even were told when to shower each day.

At Groton, Franklin met Endicott Peabody, one of the people who would have a great influence on him. As the school's founder and headmaster, and as a minister, Peabody believed in social responsibility. He expected his students to give back to their country and their fellow citizens. Peabody lived by these expectations and treated his students as family.

At first, Franklin found it difficult to make friends. He wasn't used to being around people his own age. In addition, most of the boys had been going to the school for years. At 5 feet 3 inches (160 centimeters), Franklin was too short and thin

Franklin attended classes at Groton school from 1896 to 1900.

Franklin Roosevelt, second from left, wearing a plain white sweater, played on the Groton football team in 1899.

to stand out in football, baseball, and other popular sports, even though he tried some of them. He found success in golf, tennis, boxing, and debating. He sang in the choir and participated in school politics. His personality helped as well. Charming and handsome, Franklin gradually began to fit in with the other students and make some close friends. When his fifth cousin Theodore Roosevelt was elected governor of New York, it made Franklin something of a celebrity among his fellow students.

Franklin's time at Groton wasn't without difficulties. At 16, Franklin wanted to join the Navy and help fight in the Spanish-American War. But he contracted a dangerous disease called scarlet fever. When Sara heard Franklin was ill, she rushed to Groton to be with him. Because scarlet fever is so contagious, Sara wasn't allowed in his room. However, that didn't stop her from being near her son. She placed a stepladder under his window and sat on it for hours to keep him company.

The United States fought in the Spanish-American War to gain Cuba's independence from Spain. The war lasted from April to August 1898. During the war, the United States took ownership of the Philippine Islands, Guam, and Puerto Rico.

During Franklin's final year at Groton, he enrolled in a special program. He took 15 hours of freshman-level classes at Harvard College. Then, when he enrolled as a college student at Harvard in September 1900, he only had three more years of classes to complete to earn a degree. However, Franklin chose to stay another year for graduate school, because he was elected editor in chief of the school's newspaper, *The Harvard Crimson.*

Although Franklin graduated with a B average from Groton, he proved to be less motivated at Harvard. He tended to do best in the classes he liked the most. He majored in history and government and minored in English and public speaking.

By now, Franklin had grown. At Harvard, he stood more than 6 feet 1 inch (185 centimeters) tall

The staff of The Harvard Crimson, in 1904; Franklin is in the second row (standing), fourth from the left.

but weighed less than 150 pounds (68 kilograms) and wasn't very successful in team sports. Instead, he chose to make a name for himself by participating in other activities, particularly *The Harvard Crimson*. He also started his lifelong hobby of collecting books, prints, and other items related to the Navy.

Franklin enjoyed the social scene at Harvard. His weekends were filled with dances, parties, and fancy dinners. Teddy Roosevelt had risen to vice president of the United States while Franklin attended Harvard, so the Roosevelt name carried a great deal of weight on the social scene. Friendly and handsome, Franklin made many friends.

Franklin's Harvard years were marked with sadness, too. In December 1901, during his freshman year, his 72-year-old father died.

James Roosevelt had set up a trust for each of his sons. After his father's death, Franklin would collect $6,000 each year from the trust. Springwood and the rest of James' estate went to Sara.

In the summer of 1902, Franklin traveled with his mother to Europe to help lift her spirits. While in Paris, they heard that President William McKinley had been shot. The news was shocking, but they were heartened to hear that he was expected to recover. However, by the time Franklin and Sara reached New York about two weeks later, McKinley had died. Vice President Teddy Roosevelt was now president.

With the death of William McKinley, Theodore Roosevelt became the United States' 26th president on September 14, 1901. At age 42, Teddy was the youngest man to hold that position. He was elected president on his own merits in 1904. He decided to run again in 1912 as a member of the Progressive Party, but was defeated by Democrat Woodrow Wilson.

Although Sara kept the Springwood estate that was Franklin's childhood home, she moved to an apartment in Boston to be closer to her son. While Franklin loved his mother and enjoyed having her close, she tried to run his life. Still, he would make his own decisions.

Chapter

3 FAMILY MAN

❧⌘❧

Franklin had known Eleanor Roosevelt, one of his distant cousins, all his life. Though they didn't visit often, they became reacquainted when Franklin was a junior at Harvard.

In the summer of 1902, Franklin discovered Eleanor on the same train he was riding. The two started talking and found they really enjoyed each other's company. Not knowing what others in the family might think, Franklin and Eleanor started dating but kept their relationship a secret.

On November 21, 1903, Eleanor went with Franklin to the Harvard-Yale football game. The next day, they met at Groton. After lunch, they went for a walk, and Franklin asked Eleanor to marry him. She didn't respond right away. She went to New York and

Franklin took a break with his mother, Sara, wife, Eleanor, five children, and dog in 1919.

talked to her grandmother about it. Then Eleanor was ready to give Franklin her answer. She told him yes.

Franklin shared his big news with Sara on Thanksgiving Day. But she was less than enthusiastic. His mother didn't dislike Eleanor, she just didn't want her son to marry. Both Franklin and Eleanor tried to comfort Sara by sending her letters that said she wasn't losing a son, she was gaining a daughter. Eleanor wrote:

I know just how you feel & how hard it must be, but I do so want you to learn to love me a little. You must know that I will always try to do what you wish for I have grown to love you very dearly during the past summer. It is impossible for me to tell you how I feel toward Franklin. I can only say that my one great wish is always to prove worthy of him.

Unlike Franklin, Eleanor suffered through a sad, lonely childhood. Her beautiful mother, Anna, looked at her daughter as a homely, awkward disappointment. While Eleanor's father, Elliott, loved his daughter, he struggled with alcoholism. By the time Eleanor was 10, her mother and one brother were dead from diptheria, and her father had died of alcoholism.

Sara argued that they were too young to get married. Franklin was 22, and Eleanor was 19. At Sara's suggestion, the young couple kept their engagement a secret. Sara wanted them to think more about their decision. However, their minds

Eleanor Roosevelt, Franklin's fifth cousin and future wife, visited him at Campobello Island in 1904.

were made up. Franklin and Eleanor only agreed to secrecy because they believed Sara would grow accustomed to their engagement. But she wouldn't. In fact, Sara worked to break them up.

In early 1904, Sara sent Franklin on a five-week Caribbean cruise hoping time away from Eleanor would make him change his mind. When that didn't work, Sara contacted Joseph Choate, an old family friend who was now ambassador to Great Britain. She asked him to take Franklin to London and give him

Born in Salem, Massachusetts, in 1832, Joseph Choate gained a reputation in New York as one of the finest lawyers in the country. His legal career spanned five decades and included many famous cases. In 1899, President William McKinley chose Choate as the U.S. ambassador to Great Britain, a position he held for six years. He helped strengthen the friendship between the two governments.

a job as a secretary. When Choate refused, Sara finally gave up.

In the fall of 1904, Franklin enrolled in Columbia Law School to be closer to Eleanor, who lived in New York. They married on March 17, 1905. President Teddy Roosevelt, Eleanor's uncle, gave her away.

The newlyweds lived in the Hotel Webster until Franklin completed his classes in June. Though both Franklin and Eleanor received money through trust funds, Sara paid their rent and gave them extra spending money. She also gave them a three-month honeymoon cruise and tour of Europe.

After returning from their honeymoon, the Roosevelts moved into a Manhattan home just three blocks away from Sara. Franklin went to work with a law firm.

In time, the young couple started a family. Their daughter, Anna, was born May 3, 1906. James joined the family in 1907. Franklin Jr. was born in 1909 but died of pneumonia that same year. Elliott was born in 1910, a second Franklin Jr. in 1914. and John in 1916.

Franklin and Eleanor Roosevelt, and their five children: Anna (left), James (standing), Franklin Jr. (front left), John (front middle), and Elliott

Sara took charge of raising the children, and shy Eleanor let her. Though Eleanor sometimes resented Sara, Franklin enjoyed having his mother around and particularly enjoyed her money. When the family needed a bigger home, Sara bought them one. She also made sure her own home adjoined it, so she could be with them whenever she wanted. While Franklin enjoyed his mother's money and her company, he never let her dictate his choices. He would always be his own man. Still, Sara would remain close to Franklin and his family until her death in 1941.

Though he was a busy man, Roosevelt loved his children and enjoyed his time with them. He welcomed outdoor adventures regardless of the

Roosevelt relaxed with his mother (left) and his wife at Hyde Park, New York, in 1920.

season. He spent time boating and teaching his children to swim and climb. Keeping up with their father was a challenge for the Roosevelt children. Son James remembered:

> We went sledding on a long hill leading to an area above the Hudson River. The run must have been a mile or more. Father was like a boy on those sledding expeditions. He would chase us back up the steep road so fast our lungs would ache from the cold air and heavy breathing. Summers he taught us to swim in the Rogers pond by throwing us in with rope attached to our waists.

In the evening, the Roosevelts often held family "sings." Roosevelt attacked the songs with gusto. "Father thought he was the best (singer), but he may have been the worst," James recalled.

The most festive and happy time of year was at Hyde Park at Christmas. On Christmas Eve, the Roosevelt children gathered around their father as he read *A Christmas Carol,* by Charles Dickens. The next morning, they'd scurry to Roosevelt's bedroom and discover their Christmas stockings, filled with goodies, dangling from the mantel of the fireplace. Still in pajamas and robes, the family would move to the library, where they opened their gifts. Later in the day, family and friends joined the Roosevelts for a holiday feast, complete with a turkey carved by Franklin.

Roosevelt's favorite place to be was at the family's cabin on Campobello Island. Part of the Canadian province of New Brunswick, the island measures just 12 miles (19 km) long and 3 miles (5 km) wide. He only spent a few weeks there during his vacations, but the rest of the Roosevelt family spent most of

> *Hyde Park, New York, was a popular residence for wealthy families, such as the Vanderbilts and Roosevelts. The Roosevelts' estate, Springwood, was purchased by Franklin's father, James Roosevelt, in 1866. At that time, the house consisted of 15 rooms. By the time Franklin and his mother finished updating it in 1916, it had doubled in size. They also added more than 400,000 trees to the estate.*

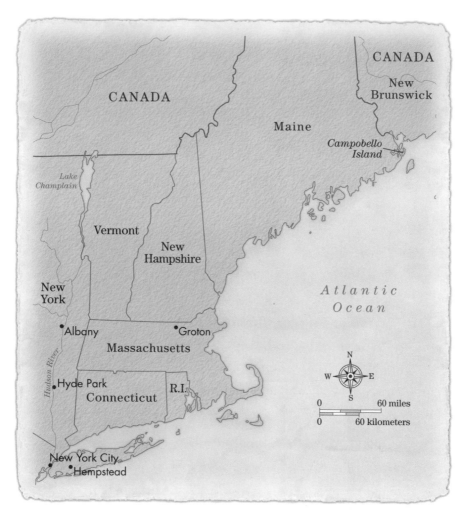

Roosevelt grew up in Hyde Park, New York, went to school in Groton, Massachusetts, and later lived in Albany, New York. He also enjoyed vacationing on Campobello Island, Canada.

their summers there.

Although the Roosevelt cabin was large, it had few modern conveniences. There were no phones, radios, or electricity. Candles and kerosene lamps provided light. The family cooked on a coal stove and kept warm with a wood-burning fireplace and coal heater.

Because the ocean water surrounding the island

remained icy all year long, Roosevelt decided to install a heated pool. Like many of his projects, it turned out to be a mess. Roosevelt liked to think of himself as quite a handyman, but few of his plans worked out. Son James later said:

> *Father tried to contribute a saltwater swimming pool to us and our neighbors, but it was a disaster. As usual, less the master builder than he believed himself to be, he had a hole dug, pipes installed and concrete poured. He devised a system whereby water would flow in from the ocean at high tide and out at low tide and be contained long enough to be heated. It never worked. The water became stagnant and stank. Over the harsh winters, the concrete cracked. The pool was not used; an eyesore, it eventually was filled in.*

Roosevelt was, however, good at carving boats from wood. With the help of his friend Louis Howe, Roosevelt not only built the boats but also sailed and raced them. He loved to sail and became an expert at guiding his boats through tricky waters. It was a hobby he passed on to his children. Roosevelt treasured the time he spent with his children. Soon, however, politics would call and the time spent with his family would be limited. ❧

4 A PATH IN POLITICS

೦⧓⧓೦

Though Sara never approved of Franklin's desire to enter politics, she agreed to finance his campaign for the New York state Senate in 1910.

Roosevelt rented a car in order to cover more territory than he could with a horse and buggy. The car was far from luxurious. It had no top or windshield, and it often left its passengers wet from rain or dusty from dry roads. But Roosevelt loved campaigning, and over the course of the 2,000 miles (3,200 km) he traveled, he became a polished public speaker. He even picked up the opening phrase "My friends," which would become his trademark.

Elected to the state Senate, Roosevelt moved his family to Albany, the capital of New York. There, away from Franklin's mother, Eleanor finally felt

Franklin Delano Roosevelt was named assistant secretary of the Navy in 1913, and served more than seven years.

Roosevelt addressed his supporters, while campaigning for senator of New York.

more at home. They rented a three-story house, which offered plenty of room for entertaining.

As a state senator, Roosevelt fought for conservation of natural resources. Unlike many freshman legislators, Roosevelt made an impact right away, mainly because of the clout his name carried. His cousin Teddy had risen through the ranks of New York politics to become president of the United States. Even though Teddy was a Republican and Franklin was a Democrat, the name Roosevelt still carried a great deal of weight in New York.

Like Teddy, Franklin had his sights set on even bigger things. When Woodrow Wilson ran for president, Roosevelt gave him his support, traveling to the Democratic National Convention in Baltimore, Maryland, in June 1912. There, in an effort to gain more national recognition, Franklin attempted to meet as many influential people from across the country as possible.

In 1912, Roosevelt ran for reelection to the Senate. However, he got off to a rocky start when he came down with typhoid fever. Knowing he'd have trouble winning the election without campaigning, Roosevelt enlisted the help of his friend Louis Howe, who now worked in newspapers.

Small and sickly all his life, Howe likely would have entered politics himself if he thought he had a chance. Knowing he couldn't campaign himself, he jumped at the chance to help Roosevelt. Howe flooded Roosevelt's Senate district with letters from the candidate and ads praising Roosevelt's accomplishments and goals for the future. The plan worked. To Roosevelt's joy, not only was he re-elected, but Wilson won the presidency.

Roosevelt headed to Washington, D.C., to attend Wilson's inauguration. While there, Roosevelt met with Secretary of the Navy Josephus Daniels, one of the men he'd met at the Democratic National Convention. Daniels asked Franklin to serve as assistant secretary of the Navy, another post his cousin Teddy had held on his rise to the top. Roosevelt didn't hesitate to give up his state Senate seat, and happily accepted the new position. He began his Washington, D.C., job March 17, 1913. He'd serve in this position for seven and one-half years.

As assistant secretary, Roosevelt dealt with the business side of the Navy. He worked on budgets, managed docks and shipyards, dealt with personnel, and attended meetings of the president's Cabinet when Daniels wasn't available. Roosevelt and Daniels made a good team. Roosevelt knew more about ships and the sea than Daniels did, but Daniels was more skilled at working with Congress to get what the Navy wanted or needed. However, Roosevelt didn't always agree with Daniels, and he wasn't afraid to make his thoughts known.

One such case arose at the beginning of World

> *Josephus Daniels was a former newspaper publisher from North Carolina. During Woodrow Wilson's administration, he was appointed secretary of the U.S. Navy. From 1933 to 1941, Daniels served as the U.S. ambassador to Mexico. He is credited with helping to improve relations between the two countries.*

War I in August 1914. Daniels believed the United States could remain neutral. Roosevelt disagreed and became upset when Daniels suggested sending Navy ships to Europe to evacuate stranded American tourists. Roosevelt believed the United States would be forced to enter the war at some point and needed to be ready for that day. Franklin voiced his frustration in a letter he sent to Eleanor:

> *Aside from the fact the tourists (female etc.) couldn't sleep in hammocks and that battleships haven't got passenger accommodations, he totally fails to grasp the fact that this war between the other powers is*

Secretary of the Navy Josephus Daniels inspected a cannon in 1919.

going inevitably to give rise to a hundred different complications in which we shall have a direct interest. Questions of refugees, of neutrality, of commerce are even now appearing and we should unquestionably gather our fleet together and get it into the highest state of efficiency.

Roosevelt continued to call for military readiness, and when his boss was out of town, he had an opportunity to get his point across. In October 1914, for example, Roosevelt issued a memo in Daniels' absence. The memo said the Navy was woefully unprepared and unable to keep 13 of its battleships running. Another 18,000 men were desperately needed. Franklin told Eleanor of the memo:

Even if it gets me into trouble I am perfectly ready to stand by it. The country needs the truth about the Army and Navy instead of a lot of the soft mush about everlasting peace which so many statesmen are handing out to a gullible public.

Roosevelt's memo made national headlines. He impressed many with his knowledge and honesty. And in the end, he was right. In early 1915, relations between the neutral United States and warring Germany grew increasingly strained. In February, Germany announced that the waters around Great

Franklin Roosevelt (far left) at the Brooklyn Navy Yard in 1914.

Britain were considered a war zone. Any ships entering the zone, including American merchant ships, would be attacked without warning. President Wilson issued his own warning to Germany. He said he would hold the German government personally responsible if any American lives were lost.

On May 7, 1915, the *Lusitania*, a British passenger ship, was torpedoed off the coast of Ireland. More than 1,000 people died, including 128 Americans. After much haggling, the German government agreed to pay a fine for American lives lost and to avoid harming passenger lines in the future. Though Wilson and many others in the government wanted to remain neutral, this incident showed them they needed to be prepared for war. In April 1917, the United States entered the war, with the Allies—Great Britain, France, and Russia—and sent its first fighting ships to Europe in early May.

With war declared, Roosevelt worked hard to prepare the Navy as best he could. He ordered more materials and equipment. He expanded training camps and asked for more recruits. In fact, he wanted to resign as assistant secretary and enlist himself, but Wilson and Daniels persuaded him to remain in his post. He could do far more in his government position

The USS Arizona was commissioned in 1916, the year before the United States entered World War I. The Arizona was later destroyed when the Japanese bombed Pearl Harbor.

than he could as an enlisted man.

The number of Navy recruits skyrocketed during the war. When war was declared, the Navy only included 67,000 men. In about six months, that number rose to 269,000. By the end of the war in 1918, nearly 500,000 people had joined the Navy, including more than 11,000 women who volunteered as so-called yeomanettes and performed office work. Among the new female recruits was Lucy Mercer, who had served as Eleanor's personal secretary.

Throughout the war, Roosevelt faced frustration. He believed Daniels needed to be more aggressive in fighting the Germans. Roosevelt showed some aggression himself. If one official didn't support a particular idea, Roosevelt would either modify his idea or keep searching until he found someone who would support him.

His idea for mining the North Sea proved to be one example of this. Roosevelt proposed creating a wall of underwater mines to keep German submarines out of the shipping lanes from Scotland to Norway. About 400,000 mines would be needed to create this wall across the 240-mile (384-km) shipping lane. When British officials said that would be impossible, Roosevelt modified his plan. A Massachusetts man named Ralph Browne had invented a new antenna mine. Unlike other mines of the day, an antenna mine didn't have to come in direct contact with a vessel. If a ship or submarine brushed up against an antenna extending from one of Browne's mines, the mine would explode. With this invention, only 100,000 antenna mines would be required to create a wall. When Daniels and Wilson supported this new plan, British officials did, too.

Construction of the wall of mines began in June 1918, but World War I ended before it could be completed. However, the mines that were in place destroyed six submarines, and fear of the mines was partially responsible for a decline in the morale of the German navy.

Born in 1865, King George V was a naval officer until the death of his older brother left him as heir to the throne. He led Great Britain through World War I and even visited the fighting front several times. He remained in power until his death in early 1936.

In July 1918, Roosevelt crossed the Atlantic to inspect naval facilities in the war zone, and he had many experiences, both good and bad. In England, he met King George V. In France, Roosevelt saw the devastated areas that had been bombed by the Germans. Twice he came under fire himself, and he witnessed a battle between Allied destroyers and a German submarine.

On the tour, Roosevelt grew ill. A bout of the flu turned into pneumonia as he traveled back to the United States in September. He felt so sick by the time he reached New York, he was taken from the boat on a stretcher to an ambulance. Eleanor quickly gathered her husband's belongings from the ship, and Roosevelt was taken to his mother's house. Among his things, Eleanor found love letters from Lucy Mercer, her former secretary. From the letters, it was clear to her that the two had been having an affair.

Lucy Mercer Rutherford was Eleanor Roosevelt's former secretary.

"The bottom dropped out of my own particular world," Eleanor later said. "I faced myself, my surroundings, my world, honestly for the first time."

Eleanor confronted Franklin with what she'd found, and Roosevelt couldn't deny the affair. After considering all their options, they decided to stay together, though for the rest of their lives they'd be more like business partners than a married couple. Eleanor could never fully forgive him. Roosevelt ended the affair immediately but remained friends with Mercer for the rest of his life. Eleanor, however, wouldn't know that until after her husband's death. ℘

5 TRIUMPH OVER TRAGEDY

Roosevelt was no stranger to failure. During his time as assistant secretary of the Navy, he sought the Democratic nomination for a U.S. Senate seat but lost to his opponent, Jim Gerard. In 1920, Roosevelt ran for vice president of the United States on the Democratic ticket with James Cox. Roosevelt campaigned hard, making nearly 1,000 speeches and appearances while crossing the country by train. But it wouldn't be enough. Promising a return to normal life after the end of World War I, the Republican ticket of Warren Harding and Calvin Coolidge won 61 percent of the popular vote. It proved to be the most lopsided loss in about 100 years.

Roosevelt turned these losses into learning experiences and opportunities for growth. The campaign

In 1920, Franklin Delano Roosevelt campaigned for vice president of the United States.

President Warren G. Harding died August 2, 1923, in San Francisco, California. The cause of his death was never determined, but he may have contracted pneumonia. Vice President Calvin Coolidge finished the remainder of Harding's term and was elected president in 1924. Coolidge chose not to run for reelection in 1928.

for vice president brought him into the national spotlight again. He also improved his speaking and other campaigning skills.

Out of politics for the time being, Roosevelt went back to practicing law. He also got involved in business, as head of the New York branch of Fidelity & Deposit Company of Maryland. He spent mornings at Fidelity and afternoons at the law office. He also remained active in political and public causes. He didn't want people to forget his name, because he knew he'd run for office again in the future.

In August 1921, Roosevelt headed to Campobello Island to join his family for a vacation. Missy LeHand, Roosevelt's secretary, worried that her boss looked tired before he left. The long journey to the island didn't help. Roosevelt manned his friend's yacht for many hours and battled the rough seas. He was rewarded with warm greetings at the Campobello dock from Eleanor, his children, and his friend Louis Howe.

Roosevelt loved the cabin at Campobello Island where he could spend time with family and friends. He went boating, fishing, and swimming. He played tennis and baseball with his children. He also took them climbing and sailing. It was on one of these sailing excursions that the Roosevelts saw a forest fire and helped extinguish it.

In 1920, an epidemic of infantile paralysis, or polio, had struck the East Coast. The disease usually targeted children. Adults generally could fight it. However, tired and weak when he came in contact

During the 1920s, polio struck many infants in the United States. The U.S. Board of Health posted signs on houses, warning people to stay away.

Polio is caused by a virus, which affects people in different ways. Some patients feel mild symptoms such as headaches, sore throats, and fevers, which often disappear after a day. Others, like Franklin Roosevelt, suffer permanent paralysis. In the 1950s, scientist Jonas Salk developed the first vaccine to help prevent polio.

with the polio virus, Roosevelt could not.

Wanting to protect Roosevelt's political future, his friend Louis Howe hid Roosevelt's condition from the media. A private railroad car took him to Presbyterian Hospital in New York. Once Roosevelt was hospitalized, Howe admitted to the media that his friend had polio, but he also shared the doctors' optimism that he would fully recover.

Roosevelt tried to get better. He spent hours straining and sweating trying to make his big toe move. In time, his arms and back grew stronger, and he was able to sit up. A month later, in October, he was released from the hospital.

In February 1922, Roosevelt began wearing leg braces, which he would wear for the rest of his life. Made of leather and steel, each brace weighed about 7 pounds (3 kg) and ran from his hip to his ankle. With crutches or support, Roosevelt could walk in the braces by moving them with the strength of his arms and upper body, but it took practice. He often tipped over and could not get back on his feet again. The crutches also caused pain in his arms.

Roosevelt wore leg braces to help him stand and walk, because polio had left his legs paralyzed.

Sara wanted her son to live in Hyde Park and run the family estate. But Eleanor and Howe had other ideas. Roosevelt had always enjoyed athletics and outdoor activities. Now unable to participate in these activities, he could have lapsed into depression. But a battered body didn't matter in the world of politics—a bright mind did, and his mind remained sharp. Eleanor was convinced he'd remain happy with his life if he could continue in politics. She and Howe vowed not only to keep up Roosevelt's spirits, but also to keep his name in front of the public. When he was ready to step back into politics, he'd have a chance to win election. Howe plotted the strategy. Roosevelt's son James later wrote:

Eleanor Roosevelt worked hard at maintaining Roosevelt's public image, and was a key to her husband's success in politics.

When father was stricken and later when it became clear that he had a long, hard road to any sort of recovery, I am convinced he would have dropped from public life completely had it not been for Louis Howe. Father was too busy with his fight for his life to think of his political future.

Eleanor overcame her shyness and began giving speeches on her husband's behalf. She and Howe attended public events and political parties. Howe also encouraged Roosevelt to write letters to other politicians to show his continued interest in the issues of the day.

In 1924, a friend suggested that Roosevelt travel to Warm Springs, Georgia. Naturally heated pools there supposedly produced miracles for some struck by paralysis. Roosevelt loved Warm Springs. In the water, his limbs didn't feel so heavy, and he could move better. He also enjoyed talking with others struggling with paralysis. Though Warm Springs didn't produce miracles for Roosevelt, it gave him a chance to exercise and relax. In time, he decided to buy the Warm Springs resort.

In Georgia, Roosevelt liked driving around in a Model-T Ford designed especially for him. Instead of foot pedals, it was rigged with ropes and pulleys he controlled with his hands. The car provided Roosevelt with another mode of transportation. He often used the vehicle to get out in public and learn what people in the community were thinking. One of his favorite places to visit was an establishment called The Cove. Even during Prohibition, Roosevelt found he could get a drink there, play a game of poker, and chat with area residents.

> The 18th Amendment to the Constitution, passed in 1920, banned the manufacture and sale of alcoholic beverages. The ban was called Prohibition. But it didn't prove very successful. Bootleggers continued to supply the country with alcohol. In 1933, the 18th Amendment was abolished. Even today, it remains the only amendment to ever be abolished.

Roosevelt gave a presidential nomination speech for Al Smith in June 1924.

With his confidence and sense of humor restored, Roosevelt faced another challenge in 1924. Howe believed it was time for him to get back into the public spotlight. Though Roosevelt wasn't a big fan of New York Governor Al Smith, Howe convinced Roosevelt to speak in support of Smith for president at the Democratic National Convention. Roosevelt ran the risk of not being able to get around the convention floor, which wasn't designed to accommodate people with physical disabilities. He also risked not being able to handle the stress of standing up and giving the speech. However, Roosevelt wouldn't let doubt or fear conquer him.

Roosevelt's 16-year-old son James helped his father get around at the convention, which was held in New York. When the time came for Roosevelt to speak, James helped him to the stage. Once there, however, Roosevelt shunned any more help. With the use of his braces and crutches, he crossed the stage on his own. The crowd watched in silence as Roosevelt, with sweat trickling down his forehead, made his way to the podium. Once there, he smiled and waved to the audience. Camera flashbulbs twinkled. The crowd burst into applause and rose in a standing ovation. Roosevelt's speech didn't gain Smith the Democratic nomination for president, which went to former congressman and ambassador John W. Davis. But the speech made Roosevelt famous. Many newspapers even declared Roosevelt should have been nominated for president. In time, he would be. ✒

6 GOVERNOR ROOSEVELT

❦

Five years after giving his speech at the Democratic National Convention, in January 1929, Roosevelt and his family moved back to Albany, New York—this time into the governor's mansion. Roosevelt had completed his successful return to politics when he was elected governor of New York in 1928.

As governor, Roosevelt worked for conservation of natural resources, pensions for the elderly, cheap electrical power for farmers, safety codes for factories, and help for the unemployed. This last task would become even more important after the stock market crash in October 1929 and the Great Depression that followed.

When the stock market crashed, thousands of U.S. citizens lost large amounts of money. People lost faith in

Franklin Delano Roosevelt smiled broadly when he heard he was leading the race for governor of New York in 1928.

The Great Depression
was an economic slump
felt around the world in
the 1930s. Banks,
factories, and other
businesses closed
in record numbers.
Droughts ravaged large
parts of the United
States mainly because
of poor farming
practices. Millions of
people lost their jobs
and homes. Poor eco-
nomic conditions in
Germany led to the rise
of Adolf Hitler and
World War II.

the economy and stopped purchasing goods and services they normally would have bought. With fewer consumers buying their products, many factories closed, and millions of people lost their jobs. Banks began to fail when people could no longer repay their loans. When banks closed, customers lost all the money they had there. The country entered the Great Depression.

While governor, Roosevelt created the Temporary Emergency Relief Administration to help provide jobs for the unemployed. The administration also made sure those in need received food, clothing, and shelter. At the time, this program seemed radical, and it took some effort to get New York legislators to approve it. Roosevelt said the relief administration needed $20 million to function. This cost would be covered by an increase in state income taxes, an unpopular thought among many lawmakers. But Roosevelt convinced them it was their responsibility to help citizens in need. He said:

> The duty of the State toward the citizen is
> the duty of the servant to its master. The

people have created it; the people, by common consent, permit its continual existence. One of these duties of the State is that of caring for those of its citizens who find themselves the victims of such adverse circumstances as makes them unable to obtain even the necessities for mere existence without the aid of others. ... To these unfortunate citizens aid must be extended by government—not as a matter of charity but as a matter of social duty.

In 1932, more than 1.5 million citizens in the state of New York were jobless. The $20 million set aside

Dorothea Lange's 1936 photo of a migrant mother and her two children captured the struggle that many U.S. citizens experienced during the Great Depression.

for relief quickly proved to be too little. Legislators saw the need was real, and they set aside even more money for the program.

Roosevelt served a total of four years—two terms—as New York's governor. Garnering 750,000 more votes than his opponent after running for reelection, Roosevelt became a natural choice to run for president in 1932. And Howe did his part to make sure of it.

"I do not see how Mr. Roosevelt can escape becoming the next presidential nominee of his party, even if no one should raise a finger to bring it about," Howe said in a press release the morning after Roosevelt's reelection. Though Roosevelt hadn't known about the press release before it was made public, he wasn't angry. He just told the media his only immediate plans were to do the best job possible as New York's governor.

While Roosevelt acted as if he wasn't really thinking about the presidency, Howe continued to make sure his friend would hold that prestigious position. In 1932, Roosevelt earned the nomination as the Democratic candidate for president at the national convention in Chicago, Illinois.

The next president would face a nation in crisis. About 17 million people were unemployed. They begged in the streets or took jobs that paid very little. Droughts and dust storms killed crops and livestock

in the country's Midwest. Many people lived in the streets, unable to afford their house payments. Republican President Herbert Hoover hadn't been able to ease the effects of the Depression, so when Roosevelt ran against him for president, people were looking for change. Roosevelt gave people hope that he could do better.

Farm machinery in South Dakota was buried during the dust storms of the 1930s.

He campaigned hard and, despite his physical disabilities, managed to travel across most of the United States. "I pledge you, I pledge myself to a new deal for the American people," Roosevelt had told the crowd at the Democratic National Convention.

Newspaper reporters picked up on the term *new deal*, and from then on, Roosevelt's plans for recovery would go by that title.

In the November election, Roosevelt managed to win 57 percent of the popular vote and 88 percent of the electoral vote. He was sworn in as president of the United States on March 4, 1933. ❧

7 THE NEW DEAL

❧

The Washington, D.C., sky was gray, and a cold wind blew on March 4, 1933. Rain poured off and on throughout the day. The dreary weather reflected the way many Americans felt at the time. With so many jobless and suffering, citizens needed hope for the future. On his first day as president, Roosevelt offered it to them in his first inaugural speech, which was widely broadcast by radio:

> *This great Nation will endure as it has endured, will revive and will prosper. So, first of all, let me assert my firm belief that the only thing we have to fear is fear itself. ... I shall ask the Congress for the one remaining instrument to meet the crisis—broad Executive Power to wage war against the emergency, as great as the*

During World War II, President Roosevelt often gave "fireside chats" on the radio.

*power that would be given me if we were
in fact invaded by a foreign foe.*

Roosevelt talked about the New Deal programs and some of his plans to help the struggling nation. He wanted to start public works programs to give people jobs, offer low-interest loans to stop home foreclosures, and fix the banking system so people's savings would remain safe. The crowd roared its approval.

President Franklin Delano Roosevelt, who was nicknamed FDR, took an approach opposite that of his predecessor. Herbert Hoover had thought helping big corporations would cause the economy to turn around. He reasoned that if large companies were healthy, they'd hire more people, who in turn would have more money to put back into the economy and help it grow. Roosevelt, on the other hand, chose to help the most downtrodden first. He knew these people needed assistance to survive and couldn't wait for the economy to improve.

As president, many of the programs Roosevelt instituted to help the nation were ones he found successful when he served as governor of New York. He utilized radio in his "fireside chats," during which he explained his new programs to the country. He called his audience "friends" and spoke in a comfortable, conversational way. People across the country gathered around their radios to hear what the president had to say. His plans gave them hope that help was on the way, even if they weren't the first to receive it.

Roosevelt's first 100 days in office included an amazing amount of activity. An emergency banking bill helped get the banking system back on its feet and protected those who had entrusted their savings there. The Federal Emergency Relief Act brought help to the unemployed, and the Civilian Conservation Corps provided jobs for 2 million young men. The Home Owners' Loan Act allowed homeowners to

Men from the Civilian Conservation Corps built a shelter on the South Mountain Reservation in New Jersey. The CCC helped unemployed U.S. citizens as part of Roosevelt's New Deal programs.

The Civilian Conservation Corps and the Public Works Administration provided training and employment to young men willing to work on conservation and public building projects around the United States. Jobs ranged from planting trees in national parks to building dams, schools, and roadways. Many of the buildings, bridges, and walkways constructed by these organizations are still in use today.

borrow money at low interest rates to help them with their mortgage payments.

In fact, many of the programs Roosevelt put into place are still being used today. The Glass-Steagall Act created the Federal Deposit Insurance Corporation (FDIC), which is an important organization that insures bank deposits. The National Industrial Recovery Act created the National Recovery Administration (NRA), whose job was to enforce codes of fair business practices developed by industry representatives. These codes controlled minimum wages allowed for workers and the maximum number of hours they could work and supported the rights of employees to join unions. Though the Supreme Court ruled the act unconstitutional in 1935, codes such as those enforced by the NRA still stand today.

The Social Security Act provided retirement funds for the elderly and financial help for needy children and the disabled. It also provided insurance for the unemployed. It continues to offer this help today.

Roosevelt also made changes in how the White

House was run. The atmosphere became less stiff and formal. Roosevelt called White House staff members by their first names or by nicknames he made up for them. He also welcomed calls from the public rather than having them redirected to other agencies. Roosevelt figured if someone felt a problem was important enough to call the White House about, then someone from the White House should be kind enough to respond. Many calls came from farmers facing foreclosures. While the White House staff often handled these calls, Eleanor took some of them herself.

Men from the Reforestation Army, part of the Civilian Conservation Corps, cleared brush from a hillside in the St. Joe National Forest in Idaho.

In fact, Eleanor became an important source of information for her husband. In Roosevelt's first year in office, Eleanor traveled about 40,000 miles (64,000 km) and reported back to her husband about what she'd seen and heard. She visited everything from hospitals to coal mines. One morning, Eleanor left the White House to visit a prison. Roosevelt hadn't seen her before she left and wondered where she'd gone. He asked her secretary, Malvina Thompson, where the first lady went.

"She's in prison, Mr. President," Thompson replied.

Eleanor Roosevelt spent much of her time on the road, talking to citizens and reporting her findings to her husband. She visited the Bear Mountain Unemployed Girls' Camp in 1933.

"I'm not surprised, but what for?" Roosevelt joked.

Roosevelt came to depend upon Eleanor's reports and seriously considered them when making decisions. He also made friends with members of the media. Along with his fireside chats on the radio, newspapers provided Roosevelt a forum for getting important information out to the public. Before the United States entered World War II, Roosevelt met with reporters twice a week. In appreciation for his openness, photographers accepted an unspoken rule: They rarely photographed Roosevelt in his wheelchair.

The 22nd Amendment to the Constitution limits how long presidents can serve. Proposed March 21, 1947, and ratified February 27, 1951, the amendment limits presidents to two terms. A president who takes over for another president and serves more than two years can only be elected once.

Not everything Roosevelt tried worked, but the U.S. public appreciated his efforts. Thousands of letters and telegrams arrived every week at the White House, thanking him for his help. In addition, the country showed its gratitude by electing him to four terms as president. No president before or since has served as long. ✑

 *Chapter* 8   WORLD WAR II

⤜⤏⤛⤜⤏⤛

About the time Roosevelt took office as president, a man named Adolf Hitler rose to power in Germany.

The German people had suffered a great deal after World War I. The Treaty of Versailles, which ended the war, forced Germany to shoulder the blame for the conflict and stripped it of lands it had conquered. The treaty also called for the country to pay reparations for war damages well beyond what it could reasonably handle. The worldwide economic crisis of the 1930s hit Germany particularly hard. People were starving and didn't know where to turn for help.

Humiliated and looking for hope, the German people believed Hitler could help them. He promised them better times and made them proud to be

Adolf Hitler became chancellor of Germany in 1933. He would prove to be one of the most brutal dictators the world has seen.

A failed artist from Austria, Adolf Hitler became Germany's chancellor on January 30, 1933. His plans for world domination and the destruction of the Jewish population were detailed in his book, Mein Kampf, which was published before he came to power. However, most who read it didn't believe such a plan would become a reality, and the book was largely ignored.

Germans again. However, Hitler's promises only extended to those he saw as "true Germans"—a master Aryan race made up of blue-eyed blondes. Those not fitting the Aryan profile, particularly those of Jewish faith, discovered Hitler planned to exterminate them in concentration camps.

Hitler dreamed of a 1,000-year Reich, or empire. He started small, testing the will of the world to stop him. The 1919 Treaty of Versailles, which had ended World War I for Germany, placed limits on the size of the German military, but slowly and quietly Hitler began building it up again. He also started taking back some of the areas that had been stripped from Germany's control.

On March 7, 1936, German troops marched into the Rhineland, an area separating Germany from France. Hitler met no resistance. With this success, he grew bolder. Other countries fell under Germany's control without any shots being fired, including Austria and Czechoslovakia. Still recovering from World War I, other European nations chose not to challenge Hitler. Not wanting another war, they

Nazi Party leader Adolf Hitler addressed an audience at a rally in 1937.

hoped the German dictator would be satisfied.

But he wasn't. On September 1, 1939, despite warnings from Great Britain and France, German troops invaded Poland. Great Britain and France came to Poland's aid. World War II had begun.

Bill Bullitt, the U.S. ambassador to France, woke Roosevelt with the news that Germany had invaded Poland. The president issued a proclamation of

The front page of London's Evening Standard *newspaper, on September 1, 1939, announced the German invasion of Poland.*

neutrality. However, even at this time Roosevelt didn't remain completely neutral in the conflict. He fought for the repeal of an arms embargo. By lifting the embargo, the United States could sell weapons to France and Great Britain. Roosevelt had no intention of selling weapons or helping the Germans in any way.

But Germany didn't care. It didn't need any help from the United States. Germany's mighty *blitzkrieg*, or lightning war, was a type of warfare in which soldiers advanced quickly, destroyed enemy lines, and were followed by bombers who finished the job. The *blitzkrieg* helped Germany to easily defeat Poland. In less than a month, the country fell into Hitler's hands. He then defeated Norway, Denmark, Belgium, Luxembourg, and Holland. By June 1940, France also fell into German hands.

Had Roosevelt had his own way, the United States would likely have entered World War II much sooner than it did. He recognized the danger Hitler posed to the world. But as president, Roosevelt had to wait until other Americans began to see it, too. For now, the majority of the country wanted to remain neutral, despite pleas for help from Great Britain.

In spite of the U.S. policy of neutrality, the country began preparing itself for the possibility of war. Just a week before Roosevelt was elected to a third term as president in 1940, the first American soldiers were drafted. Though the United States wasn't yet in the fight, these soldiers began training. It quickly became clear how unprepared the country was for battle. Because of a lack of equipment, recruits trained using broomsticks instead of rifles, and sawhorses instead of machine guns.

The president promised these new troops wouldn't be sent into a foreign war. He told the public he was building up the country's military strength to make others think before threatening the

United States. He also asked other countries to help Great Britain and others fighting the Axis powers, as Germany and its allies were called. Roosevelt reasoned that by helping Great Britain with weapons and other supplies, the United States might not need to send its own troops into the conflict. Roosevelt explained in one of his fireside chats:

> *There is far less chance for the United States getting into war if we do all we can to support the nations defending themselves against attack by the Axis than if we acquiesce in their defeat, submit tamely to Axis victory, and wait our turn to be the object of an attack in another war later on.*

Roosevelt's Lend-Lease Program, started in March 1941, allowed the United States to aid Great Britain, the Soviet Union, and other Allied nations by letting them borrow supplies. These nations desperately needed the supplies but were approaching a time when they wouldn't be able to pay for them. Great Britain, for example, held less than $2 billion in cash but had orders in American factories amounting to around $5 billion. Through the Lend-Lease Program, Great Britain could get the supplies it needed without having to worry about paying for them. In his typical style, Roosevelt explained the Lend-Lease Program to the media:

Suppose my neighbor's home catches on fire, and I have a length of garden hose four or five hundred feet away. If he can take my garden hose and connect it up with his hydrant, I may help him put out the fire. Now what do I do? I don't say to him before that operation, "Neighbor, my garden hose cost me fifteen dollars; you have to pay me fifteen dollars for it." No! What is the transaction that goes on? I don't want fifteen dollars—I want my garden hose after the fire is over.

French officers inspected their troops, who stood in front of newly-acquired American tanks in World War II. The tanks were provided to them through Roosevelt's Lend-Lease program.

Before the end of the war, the United States provided Allied forces with more than $50 billion in goods and services through the Lend-Lease Program. But the Allies wanted more. They wanted U.S. participation in the battles. Soon they would get just that. ℘

9 AMERICA ENTERS THE WAR

⁓⧉⁓

Roosevelt had communicated with British Prime Minister Winston Churchill by phone and letters. The two finally met in person on August 9, 1941, in Placentia Bay, off the coast of Newfoundland.

They liked each other right away and became lifelong friends, but that didn't mean their first face-to-face meeting didn't include any arguments. Churchill hoped to persuade Roosevelt to join the fight against Germany. Churchill feared for the future of his country and didn't want to see it fall to Hitler. Churchill also wanted the president to warn Japan, one of Germany's allies, against any further expansion.

While Roosevelt sympathized with Churchill and the British, he said he couldn't commit his country to

On June 6, 1944—D-Day—Allied troops landed on the beaches of Normandy, France, to liberate western Europe from the Germans.

fighting. He would, however, send a sharply worded letter to Japan. But the letter had little effect. Within months, Japan would bring the United States into the war. When Japanese planes bombed Pearl Harbor, Hawaii, Roosevelt addressed Congress:

> *Yesterday, December 7, 1941—a date which will live in infamy—the United States was suddenly and deliberately attacked by naval and air forces of the Empire of Japan. I ask that the Congress declare that since the unprovoked and dastardly attack by Japan on Sunday, December 7th, a state of war has existed between the United States and the Japanese Empire.*

The United States was surprised by the attack on Pearl Harbor. One hundred and eighty ships were anchored in the harbor at the time, including eight battleships, which were the main targets of the Japanese bombers. More than 20 ships and 300 American planes were damaged or destroyed in the attack. Nearly 2,400 Americans were killed and more than 1,000 suffered injuries.

Congress agreed and declared war on Japan, as did Great Britain. Three days later, Germany and Italy declared war on the United States in support of Japan.

Roosevelt whipped up the U.S. war machine. In his State of the Union address in 1942, he called for the production of 60,000 planes, 25,000 tanks, 20,000 anti-aircraft guns, and merchant vessels to replace those sunk by German

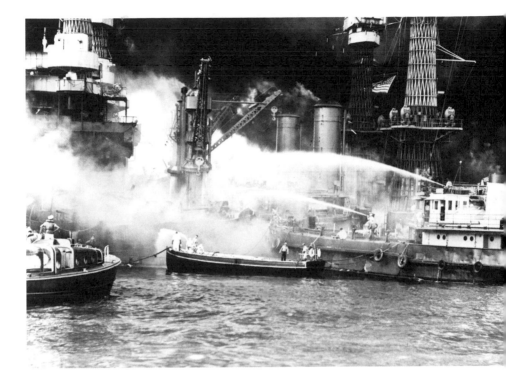

The USS West Virginia *burns in Pearl Harbor on the day of the attack.*

submarines. The next year Roosevelt raised these figures to 125,000 planes, 75,000 tanks, and 35,000 guns. By the war's end, U.S. factories and shipyards had produced nearly 300,000 airplanes, more than 86,000 tanks, more than 72,000 ships, 8.5 million rifles, and 14 million tons (12.6 million metric tons) of ammunition and bombs.

In 1942, following the attack on Pearl Harbor, Roosevelt signed an executive order that sent 110,000 Japanese-Americans to detention camps. Though about two-thirds of them were American citizens, hatred and fear toward people with Japanese

Adolf Hitler established Dachau, his first concentration camp, near Munich in early 1933. At first, Dachau served as a place to imprison his enemies. In time, a network of concentration camps was built to carry out the "Final Solution," Hitler's plan to exterminate Europe's Jewish population. Around 6 million Jewish men, women, and children were murdered. In addition, Hitler had millions of others killed, including gypsies, communists, homosexuals, people who were mentally or physically disabled, and religious leaders of varying faiths.

backgrounds had hit the United States. With no reason to believe any of these people were spies or disloyal to the United States in any way, U.S. officials removed Japanese-Americans from their homes and imprisoned them in remote desert areas. They remained there until the end of the war.

Another tragedy continued in Europe. Hitler was killing millions of Jews in concentration camps. None of the Allies, including the United States, made any effort to end this suffering until near the war's end. Appeals by Jews and humanitarians to bomb rail lines leading to death camps went unheard. Allied leaders said the Jews would be better helped in the long run by the defeat of Germany.

Defeating Germany remained Roosevelt's first priority, even though the Japanese had brought the United States into the war. After a January 1943 meeting with Churchill in Casablanca, Morocco, Roosevelt announced that nothing short of Germany's unconditional surrender would be accepted.

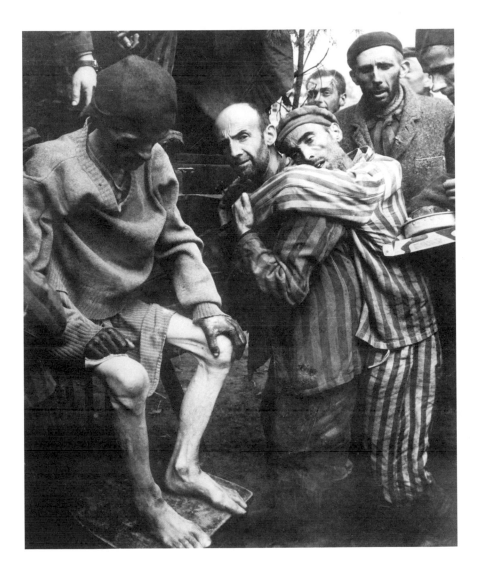

From November 28 to December 2 of that same year, Roosevelt met in Tehran, Iran, with Churchill and Soviet dictator Joseph Stalin to discuss the Allied strategy. Already the Soviets were beating back the Germans on the eastern front. The United States and

By 1945, most surviving prisoners in Hitler's concentration camps throughout Germany were starving to death.

SOVIET UNION
MONG.
CHINA
JAPAN
Pacific Ocean
Pearl Harbor
AUSTRALIA
UNITED STATES

Extent of Axis control, 1942
Map shows boundaries of 1939.

Arkhangelsk

Atlantic Ocean

NORWAY
SWEDEN
FINLAND
SOVIET UNION
Leningrad
EST.
Moscow
LAT.
LITH.

UNITED KINGDOM
North Sea
DEN.
IRELAND
NETH.
London
Berlin
Warsaw
POLAND
BEL.
GERMANY
Paris
SLOV.
SWITZ.
FRANCE
HUN.
Vichy
ROMANIA
Yalta
Black Sea
ITALY
YUGO.
BULG.
PORT.
Rome
ALB.
SPAIN
GREECE
TURKEY
SYRIA
Mediterranean Sea
PALESTINE
MOROCCO
TUNISIA
ALGERIA
LIBYA
EGYPT

N W E S

0   400 miles
0   400 kilometers

During World War II, the Axis powers of Germany, Italy, and Japan took control of parts of Europe, Asia, and Africa.

Great Britain continued to fight the Germans from the west after defeating the Axis powers in North Africa and Italy.

A turning point came on June 6, 1944. For months, the Allies had been planning to attack German troops in France. On what was called D-Day, 2,700

Allied vessels carried more than 170,000 soldiers across the English Channel to Normandy. The attack surprised the Germans, but they fought back fiercely. Through one of the bloodiest battles of the war, the Allies secured the beaches and Normandy, allowing 1 million soldiers, equipment, and supplies to flow into France. It was only a matter of time before soldiers from the west would fight their way into Germany.

In February 1945, the end of World War II appeared near. Roosevelt, Churchill, and Stalin met in Yalta, Ukraine, to discuss how to proceed once peace was restored. Churchill wanted a free, democratic Europe. Stalin wanted to protect his borders so he wouldn't face attack again. Roosevelt wanted to finish the war with Japan and was willing to compromise with Stalin to secure peace.

The Soviets had the largest army in Europe, and Stalin used that fact to get his way at Yalta. Roosevelt and Churchill agreed to return Soviet prisoners of war to their homeland. Soviet troops were also given permission to remain in Poland until order was restored and free elections could be arranged. Stalin agreed that could be accomplished quickly. ❧

10 FINAL DAYS

❧⋆❧

World War II drained away much of Roosevelt's energy. Often he regained his vigor by spending time with family and friends. However, he was often alone these days. Eleanor kept busy with speaking engagements and travel. Though they held deep affection for one another, the rift caused by his affair with Lucy Mercer never really healed. Although Roosevelt wanted to be as close to Eleanor as he was before the affair, Eleanor never felt the same toward her husband as she had in the beginning of their marriage.

Their children were grown and now had responsibilities of their own. In addition, many of those closest to him had died, including his mother, his secretary, and his adviser and friend Louis Howe.

President Franklin Delano Roosevelt's final term was cut short by his death on April 12, 1945.

91 ❧

Elizabeth Shoumatoff, of New York, was a well-known and respected watercolor artist. Born in 1888, she lived until 1980. She never completed the portrait of Franklin Roosevelt she was painting before he died. Titled Unfinished Portrait, the work can be seen at the Little White House, Franklin Delano Roosevelt's Warm Springs home.

A tired Roosevelt headed to Warm Springs on March 30, 1945. The morning of April 12, Roosevelt awoke with a stiff neck and headache. Cousins visiting him, however, thought he looked remarkably well. Lucy Mercer also was visiting, as was the artist Elizabeth Shoumatoff, who was there to paint the president's portrait.

In the morning, Franklin worked as Shoumatoff painted. The president appeared to be in good spirits, but he couldn't shake his headache. In the early afternoon, he slumped in his chair. Eleanor, who was in Washington, D.C., received a phone call that Franklin had fainted. Because she was told his condition didn't appear serious, she went on with plans to attend a meeting. A couple of hours later, Roosevelt died of a cerebral hemorrhage. He was 63 years old.

In Great Britain, a sad Churchill broke the news to Parliament. In the United States, thousands of mourners lined the streets of Washington, D.C., to say goodbye to President Roosevelt. His funeral was held in the White House on April 14. As the ceremony began, two minutes of silence were observed across the country in his honor. Traffic lights stayed on yellow; trains stopped on their tracks. After the funeral, the president's body was taken to Hyde Park, New York, for burial.

Roosevelt (left) with Vice President Harry Truman in 1944, less than one year before Roosevelt's death.

In Europe and Asia, World War II raged on, though it was nearing its end. Vice President Harry Truman stepped in as president and began leading the U.S. efforts. Churchill worried Truman may have been kept in the dark on many issues, including the Manhattan Project, a U.S. program to build the world's first atomic bomb. Indeed, until he became president, Truman didn't even know such a program existed. Yet he would be the one to issue the order to drop atomic bombs on Japan, ending World War II with Japan's surrender on September 2, 1945. Germany had already surrendered on May 7, less than a month after Roosevelt's death.

Harry Truman served as vice president only 83 days before Franklin Roosevelt died. He was elected president on his own merits in 1948. During his time in office, the spread of communism ranked as one of America's greatest fears. Truman developed the Truman Doctrine, which promised aid to countries that resisted the spread of communism.

Today, Roosevelt's legacy is still part of Americans' everyday lives—in programs such as Social Security and others that help factory workers, farmers, and all people in the workforce. Though born into wealth, he championed the causes of working men and women.

Greatly loved and respected, Roosevelt continues to be memorialized. His name graces school buildings and bridges, including the Franklin D. Roosevelt Memorial Bridge, which connects Lubec,

Elizabeth Shoumatoff's unfinished portrait of Franklin Delano Roosevelt

Maine, with Campobello Island. He is remembered as one of the nation's greatest presidents, a man who helped keep the country together in times of great crisis—a leader who brought the United States out of the Great Depression and to the brink of victory in World War II. ❧

ROOSEVELT'S LIFE

1886

Begins attending
Groton, a
Massachusetts
prep school

1882

Born in Hyde
Park, N.Y., on
January 30

1903

Graduates from
Harvard College

1880

1881

The first Japanese
political parties
are formed

1901

First exhibition
of Pablo Picasso
opens

1903

Brothers Orville
and Wilbur Wright
successfully fly a
powered airplane

WORLD EVENTS

1905

Marries Eleanor
Roosevelt on
March 17

1907

Graduates from
Columbia Law
School; joins the
law firm of Carter,
Ledyard and Milburn

1911

Begins term in
the New York
state Senate

1906

A Canadian-born
physicist, Reginald
Fessenden, makes the
first successful radio
broadcast—a poetry
reading, a violin solo,
and a speech

1909

The National
Association for
the Advancement
of Colored People
(NAACP) is founded

ROOSEVELT'S LIFE

1912

Runs successfully for
second term in New
York state Senate

1913

Resigns from Senate
after being named
assistant secretary of
the Navy

1912

The *Titanic*
sinks on its
maiden voyage;
more than 1,500
people die

1913

Henry Ford begins to
use standard assembly
lines to produce
automobiles

1914

Archduke Franz
Ferdinand is assas-
sinated, launching
World War I (1914–
1918)

WORLD EVENTS

1920

Runs unsuccessfully for vice president of the United States on a ticket with James Cox

1921

Stricken with polio while vacationing at Campobello Island

1924

Speaks on behalf of Al Smith for president at the Democratic National Convention June 24 in New York

1920

1920

American women get the right to vote

1923

French actress Sarah Bernhardt dies

ROOSEVELT'S LIFE

1928

Elected
governor of
New York

1932

Elected president of
the United States; he
would be reelected in
1936, 1940, and 1944

1933

Delivers first
"fireside chat"

1930

1926

A.A. Milne
publishes
Winnie the Pooh

1930

Designs for the first
jet engine are sub-
mitted to the Patent
Office in Britain

1933

Nazi leader Adolf
Hitler is named
chancellor of
Germany

WORLD EVENTS

1941

Establishes Lend-
Lease program to aid
European allies; asks
Congress to declare
war on Japan

1942

Orders Japanese-
Americans to be
placed in intern-
ment camps

1945

Attends Yalta
Conference in
February; dies on
April 12

1940

1939

German troops invade
Poland; Britain and
France declare war on
Germany; World War II
(1939–1945) begins

1945

The United
Nations is
founded

NAME: Franklin Delano Roosevelt

DATE OF BIRTH: January 30, 1882

BIRTHPLACE: Hyde Park, New York

FATHER: James Roosevelt (1828-1900)

MOTHER: Sara Delano Roosevelt (1854-1941)

EDUCATION: Harvard College and Columbia Law School

SPOUSE: Anna Eleanor Roosevelt (1884-1962)

DATE OF MARRIAGE: March 1905

CHILDREN: Anna (1906–1975)
James (1907–1991)
Franklin Jr. (1909–1909)
Elliott (1910–1990)
Franklin Jr. (1914–1988)
John (1916–1981)

DATE OF DEATH: April 12, 1945

PLACE OF BURIAL: Hyde Park

Further Reading

Ambrose, Stephen. *The Good Fight: How World War II Was Won.* New York: Antheneum Books for Young Readers, 2001.

Grant, Reg. *The Great Depression.* San Diego, Calif.: Lucent Books, 2005.

Grapes, Bryan J. *Franklin D. Roosevelt.* San Diego, Calif.: Greenhaven Press, 2001.

Uschan, Michael V. *The Importance of Franklin D. Roosevelt.* San Diego: Lucent Books, 2002.

Look for more Signature Lives

books about this era:

Andrew Carnegie: *Captain of Industry*
ISBN 0-7565-0995-5

Carrie Chapman Catt: *A Voice for Women*
ISBN 0-7565-0991-2

Henry B. Gonzalez: *Congressman of the People*
ISBN 0-7565-0996-3

J. Edgar Hoover: *Controversial FBI Director*
ISBN 0-7565-0997-1

Langston Hughes: *The Voice of Harlem*
ISBN 0-7565-0993-9

Douglas MacArthur: *America's General*
ISBN 0-7565-0994-7

Wilma Mankiller: *Chief of the Cherokee Nation*
ISBN 0-7565-1600-5

Eleanor Roosevelt: *First Lady of the World*
ISBN 0-7565-0992-0

Elizabeth Cady Stanton: *Social Reformer*
ISBN 0-7565-0990-4

Gloria Steinem: *Champion of Women's Rights*
ISBN 0-7565-1587-4

On the Web

For more information on *Franklin Delano Roosevelt,* use FactHound.

1. Go to *www.facthound.com*
2. Type in a search word related to this book or this book ID: 0756515866.
3. Click on the *Fetch It* button. FactHound will fetch the best Web sites for you.

Historic Sites

Franklin D. Roosevelt Presidential Library and Museum
4079 Albany Post Road
Hyde Park, NY 12538
845/486-7770
Exhibits featuring items from Franklin D. Roosevelt's life

FDR's Little White House
401 Little White House Road
Georgia Highway 85 Alternate
Warm Springs, GA 31830
706/655-5870
Vacation home and new museum feature personal items from Roosevelt's life

acquiesce
give in

aggressive
bold

Aryan
Term used by Nazis to describe a supposed master race of non-Jewish, pure-blooded Germans with blond hair and blue eyes

bootleggers
those individuals, during Prohibition, who produced and sold alcohol illegally

chloroform
a toxic liquid once used to ease pain or make a person unconscious for surgery

clout
influence

embargo
an act by a government stopping trade to or from another country

exterminate
to wipe out or destroy

fatigue
great tiredness

gullible
easily fooled

humanitarians
people who want to help end the suffering of others

Glossary

inauguration
a ceremony at which a president is sworn
into office

mortgage
a loan from a bank to buy a house or a piece
of land

quarantine
the keeping of a person or animal away from
others to stop the spread of disease

recruits
newly enlisted soldiers or sailors

reparations
payment of damages

stagnant
polluted because of a lack of movement

typhoid fever
a dangerous, contagious disease caused by germs
in food or water

Chapter 1

Page 10, line 3: Nathan Miller. *F.D.R.: An Intimate History.* Garden City, N.Y.: Doubleday & Co., 1983, p. 183.

Page 11, line 8: Ibid.

Page 12, line 23: James Roosevelt. *My Parents: A Differing View.* Chicago: Playboy Press, 1976, p. 72.

Chapter 2

Page 18, line 10: *F.D.R.: An Intimate History*, p. 7.

Chapter 3

Page 30, line 10: Ibid., p. 48.

Page 34, line 5: *My Parents: A Differing View*, pp. 46–47.

Page 35, line 4: Ibid., p. 48.

Page 37, line 6: Ibid., p. 53.

Chapter 4

Page 43, line 9: *F.D.R.: An Intimate History*, p. 119.

Page 44, line 16: Ibid., p. 124.

Page 49, line 15: Ibid., p. 152.

Chapter 5

Page 56, line 17: *My Parents: A Differing View*, p. 76.

Chapter 6

Page 62, line 26: *F.D.R.: An Intimate History*, pp. 254–255.

Page 64, line 10: Ibid., p. 246.

Page 65, line 10: *My Parents: A Differing View*, p. 136.

Chapter 7

Page 67, line 9: *F.D.R.: An Intimate History*, pp. 4–5.

Page 72, line 11: Ibid., p. 359.

Chapter 8

Page 80, line 8: Ibid., p. 459.

Page 81, line 1: Ibid., p. 460.

Chapter 9

Page 84, line 6: Ibid., p. 380.

Black, Conrad. *Franklin Delano Roosevelt: Champion of Freedom.* New York: Public Affairs, 2003.

Burns, James. *Roosevelt: The Soldier of Freedom.* New York: Harcourt, Brace, 1970.

Burns, James. *Roosevelt: The Lion and the Fox.* New York: Harcourt, Brace, 1956.

Freidel, Frank Burt. *Franklin D. Roosevelt: a Rendezvous With Destiny.* Boston: Little, Brown, 1990.

Miller, Nathan. *F.D.R.: An Intimate History.* Garden City, N.Y.: Doubleday & Company, 1983.

Roosevelt, James. *My Parents: A Differing View.* Chicago: Playboy Press, 1976.

Schlesinger, Arthur M., Jr. *The Coming of the New Deal: 1933–1935, the Age of Roosevelt, Volume II.* New York: Houghton Mifflin, 2003.

Brenda Haugen started in the newspaper business and had a career as an award-winning journalist before finding her niche as an author. Since then, she has written and edited many books, most of them for children. A graduate of the University of North Dakota in Grand Forks, Brenda lives in North Dakota with her family.

Image Credits